Serving on a Jury

SARAH DE CAPUA

Children's Press®
An Imprint of Scholastic Inc.
New York Toronto London Auckland Sydney
Mexico City New Delhi Hong Kong
Danbury, Connecticut

Content Consultant
Margaret Heubeck
Youth Leadership Initiative Director of Instruction
University of Virginia Center for Politics
Charlottesville, Virginia

Library of Congress Cataloging-in-Publication Data

De Capua, Sarah.
  Serving on a jury/by Sarah De Capua.
    p. cm.—(A true book)
  Includes bibliographical references and index.
  ISBN-13: 978-0-531-26042-5 (lib. bdg.)
  ISBN-13: 978-0-531-26214-6 (pbk.)
  1. Jury—United States—Juvenile literature. I. Title.
  KF8972.D425 2012
  347.73'752—dc23   2012000628

All rights reserved. Published in 2013 by Children's Press, an imprint of Scholastic Inc.
Printed in China 62
SCHOLASTIC, CHILDREN'S PRESS, A TRUE BOOK™, and associated logos are trademarks and/or registered trademarks of Scholastic Inc.
1 2 3 4 5 6 7 8 9 10 R 22 21 20 19 18 17 16 15 14 13

Front cover: Attorney addresses a jury

Back cover: Blindfolded Lady Justice balances the scales of truth and fairness

Find the Truth!

Everything you are about to read is true *except* for one of the sentences on this page.

Which one is **TRUE**?

T or F A person must be at least 18 years old to serve as a juror.

T or F A juror can use social media during a trial.

Find the answers in this book.

Contents

The jury foreperson shares a jury's decision.

4 Hearing the Case

Can jurors go home each night during a trial? **31**

5 Reaching a Verdict

Who can be the jury foreperson? **39**

27. Have you ever served on a jury before? ____ Yes ____ No
If you have served on a jury before, please answer the following:
   a. Please provide the following information for each case in which you served:
   Year   Civil or Criminal   Verdict Reached (Yes/No)
   _____
   _____
   _____

   b. Were you ever the foreperson? ____ Yes ____ No
   c. Have you ever served on a GRAND JURY before? ____ Yes ____ No
   If yes, please describe where and when: _____
28. Have you or a family member ever made any type of claim for money damages?
   ____ Yes ____ No
   If yes, please explain: _____
29. Have you ever been involved in a lawsuit (other than divorce proceedings), including giving a deposition?
   ____ Yes ____ No
   If yes, were you: ____ The plaintiff ____ The defendant
   ____ Witness ____ Other
   Please explain: _____
   _____
   _____

In the United States, a jury must have at least six members.

CHAPTER 1

A Jury's Duty

What do you know about juries? Maybe you have read books, seen movies, or watched TV programs with exciting courtroom drama. If you read newspapers or watch news broadcasts on TV, you have probably heard about real-life trials and the decisions juries make. Do you want to know more about the work a jury does? Read on!

Juries are an important part of the U.S. justice system.

Important People

The members of a jury listen to the facts presented during a court trial. After all of the facts have been presented, the jury decides who is right or wrong, or whether someone is guilty. The members of a jury are called jurors. Serving on a jury is an important responsibility of being a U.S. citizen.

Jurors must pay careful attention to the details of a trial.

Today, U.S. juries usually include 12 people who must all agree on a decision.

Modern court systems are based on the ideas of the ancient Greeks.

The Roots of Jury Trials

The ancient Greeks were the first people to have trials by jury. This system was first used around 400 BCE. In ancient Greece, between 101 and 2,001 jurors decided on each trial's outcome. This decision was called a **verdict**. The Greeks believed there should be an odd number of jurors. This was to prevent a tie when reaching a verdict.

The Greeks had a set of rules to make sure a jury's decision was fair. For example, dishonest citizens were not allowed to serve. This rule is still in use today.

The English government began holding jury trials in 1066. When English colonists came to North America in the 1600s, they brought this system with them. In 1776, the colonies became the United States. Juries were an important part of the new nation's judicial system.

English settlers brought their justice system when they established North American colonies in the 1600s.

Secret Ballot

Secret ballots are votes that are cast without anyone knowing how anyone else voted. In ancient Greece, verdicts were reached by secret ballot. When the votes were counted, the decision that received the most votes became the jury's verdict. In the United States today, verdicts are not generally determined by secret ballot. However, some juries vote by secret ballot before they begin discussing a verdict. Jurors write their votes on slips of paper and one person collects and counts them. This can give jurors an idea of the jury's overall opinion.

Jurors must assume that each person is innocent until proven guilty.

Criminal trials are a fair way to decide whether an accused person is guilty of committing a crime.

Types of Jury Trials

In the United States, there are two kinds of jury trials. One kind is the criminal trial. These are often shown in movies and on TV. Criminal trials involve people who have been accused of committing crimes, such as theft or assault. If the jury reaches a guilty verdict, the criminal is punished. Punishments can include fines, prison time, or even death. The punishment depends on the state in which the case is tried.

Civil trials are slightly different. They help settle conflicts between people. A civil trial is held when one person brings a lawsuit against another. For example, someone who is injured in a car accident might sue the driver who caused the accident. If the lawsuit is successful, the guilty person must usually pay money to the person who filed the suit.

Civil trials do not involve criminal charges, but they can still have serious consequences for the people involved.

New citizens
often wave flags
at the end of
the citizenship
ceremony.

CHAPTER 2

Meeting the Requirements

In the United States, the rules for who can serve on a jury are determined by each state. However, a person must be a U.S. citizen to serve on a jury anywhere in the country. Citizens include people who were born in the United States and those who have been **naturalized**. Naturalized citizens were born in another country, moved to the United States to live permanently, and then became U.S. citizens.

← Immigrants usually must live in the United States at least five years before gaining citizenship.

15

People with serious criminal records cannot serve as jurors.

Becoming a Juror

Jurors in the United States must be at least 18 years old. They must be able to understand English so they can understand what the people involved in the case are saying. Also, jurors must be upstanding citizens. Upstanding citizens are people who do not have a history of legal trouble. Some states have other requirements that must be met before a person can serve as a juror.

Computers help determine who is called for jury service. Computers search databases that contain driver's licenses, voter registrations, and tax return files. The search brings up names of community members who meet the requirements for jury service. In many states, notices are mailed to the people whose names are chosen. The notice states when and where the person should report for jury duty. Employers are generally required to excuse employees who have jury duty from work.

It is illegal to ignore a notice of jury duty.

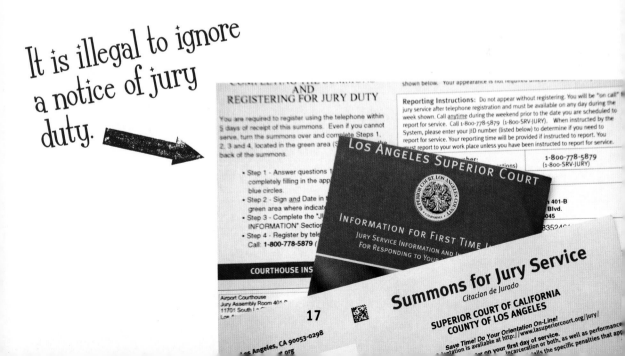

Being Excused

Members of the military are often excused from jury service

What happens if a person can't report for jury duty? **Potential** jurors can be excused from jury service, but they must have a good reason. Serious illnesses, vision or hearing problems, and demanding jobs are among the accepted reasons.

Firefighters and others with demanding jobs are often excused from serving on a jury.

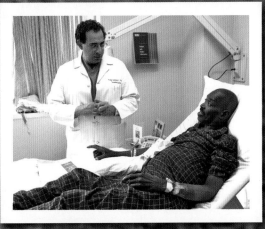

The elderly and those with serious illnesses are also excused from jury service.

Some states excuse people who are older than 70 from jury duty. The juror must offer detailed proof that his or her claim is true. The court usually excuses that person from jury duty, but he or she may receive another notice a few months or years later.

Jurors must sometimes wait many hours to find out if they have been selected for a case.

CHAPTER 3

Choosing the Jury

Not all people who receive notices to report for jury duty end up serving as jurors. Up to 300 people might be summoned to appear at the courthouse on the day a trial is scheduled to begin. They sit in a waiting room until a court clerk appears. Sometimes they are given a slip of paper with a number on it.

Potential jurors can bring work or reading materials to pass the time while waiting.

Potential jurors must listen carefully to find out if their numbers or names have been called.

Making the Cut

In most places, the clerk reads the numbers or names of people chosen for the next step in the jury selection process. This usually includes about 30 people. The lawyers and judge for the case will later narrow down this number. A person whose name or number is not called may leave the courthouse. That person will receive credit for jury service, even though he or she did not get picked for the jury.

The people who are chosen usually fill out a form. This form asks them about their habits and opinions on certain issues. For example, they may be asked to describe what kinds of books they read, what their hobbies are, or what they think about the death penalty. They turn in the forms to the court clerk, who gives the forms to the lawyers for the case.

Sometimes the juror questionnaire can be filled out online.

27. Have you ever served on a jury before?
_____ Yes _____ No
If you have served on a jury before, please answer the following:
  a. Please provide the following information for each case in which you served:

Year   Civil or Criminal   Verdict Reached (Yes/No)
_____
_____
_____
_____
_____

  b. Were you ever the foreperson? _____ Yes _____ No
  c. Have you ever served on a GRAND JURY before? _____ Yes _____ No
     If yes, please describe where and when: _____

28. Have you or a family member ever made any type of claim for money damages?
_____ Yes _____ No
If yes, please explain: _____

29. Have you ever been involved in a lawsuit (other than divorce proceedings), including giving a deposition?
_____ Yes _____ No
If yes, were you: _____ The plaintiff _____ The defendant
                 _____ Witness   _____ Other
Please explain:
_____
_____
_____

6

Next, the potential jurors are brought into the courtroom, where the case's judge and lawyers are waiting. A judge is someone who pays close attention to the case's arguments and makes sure lawyers and jurors follow proper legal procedures. He or she ensures the trial is fair for both sides.

The judge is in charge of making sure the trial is conducted fairly.

The defendant (center) sits at a table with his lawyers.

In a civil trial, the **plaintiff** is the side that has brought the lawsuit to court. In a criminal trial, the city, county, or state where the crime took place serves as the plaintiff.

The **defendant** is the person who is being sued or accused of a crime. Each side is represented by one or more lawyers.

Before the trial begins, the judge outlines important information for the potential jurors.

Court reporters record everything that is said in court.

Once the potential jurors enter the courtroom, the judge explains the basic facts of the case. He describes the crime that was committed and tells the jurors when and where it happened. He also mentions about how long the trial is likely to last. Most trials last a few days or less, though some can last several months or even years.

Narrowing Down the Jury

After the judge is done talking, lawyers from each side interview each of the potential jurors. The questions are based on the forms the jurors filled out earlier. The judge sometimes asks questions, as well, to ensure that each juror will provide a fair trial. This process is known as **voir dire**, which is taken from Old French words meaning "to speak the truth."

Lawyers and judges both ask questions during voir dire.

The lawyers for both sides are allowed to excuse a certain number of jurors during the voir dire process. Questioning can take several hours. During this time, many potential jurors are dismissed. For example, if a person knows anything about the case, or has formed opinions about it based on news reports, he or she is excused. This is because they are considered **biased**.

Lawyers try to dismiss the jurors who would most likely believe their clients to be guilty.

The selected jurors sit together in a box near the front of the courtroom.

Jurors are usually paid a small amount of money for each day of jury service.

After all the jurors and some alternates have been selected, the questioning is completed. Alternates are extra jurors who can serve if a juror must leave the trial because of an illness or other unexpected emergency. Once the jury has been selected, the trial can begin.

Lawyers ask witnesses
important questions
about the case.

CHAPTER 4

Hearing the Case

During the trial, the lawyer for the plaintiff is called the **prosecutor**. The prosecution and the defense each present evidence to support their arguments during the trial. The jurors pay close attention to the evidence and listen to each side's claims. Their most important responsibility is to be fair and open-minded. Jurors must listen to all of the facts before developing their opinions.

In some places, jurors are allowed to take notes during a trial.

Winners and Losers

During the trial, jury members must keep in mind what sort of decision they will eventually need to make. In a criminal trial, the jury's job is to decide whether or not the defendant is guilty. In some cases, the jury will also be expected to suggest a punishment if the defendant is found guilty. Often, the judge decides the punishment.

Jurors must decide whether criminal defendants are guilty or innocent.

At the end of a civil trial, the jury announces which side has won.

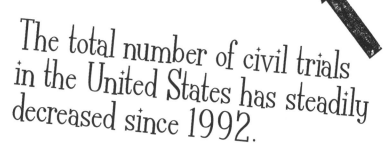

The total number of civil trials in the United States has steadily decreased since 1992.

During civil trials, a jury must choose whether the plaintiff or the defendant wins the lawsuit. If it decides that the plaintiff is the winner, it must also decide on a settlement. This is how much money the defendant would have to pay the plaintiff.

Following the Rules

While the trial is going on, jurors are not allowed to talk about the case. They cannot discuss it with one another or with family members or friends. While in the courtroom, jurors must turn off their cell phones or laptop computers. They cannot send tweets or post to their Facebook, MySpace, or other social media pages, either.

A Timeline of Juries

400 BCE
Ancient Greeks are among the first people to hold trials by jury.

1066 CE
Trials by jury begin in England.

Jurors who do not follow the rules are removed from the case and replaced by alternates. In some trials, this means that an entire new jury must be selected and the trial must be started over.

During trials that last for more than one day, jurors are usually allowed to return home once the day's activities are completed. This may be around 4:00 or 5:00 p.m. The trial usually continues the following morning.

1600s
English colonists bring the jury system to North America.

1791
The U.S. Constitution, which guarantees the right to a trial by jury, is adopted.

Jurors could be unfairly influenced if they were allowed to read newspapers.

Jurors are not allowed to return home during all trials, though. Sometimes they are **sequestered**. Sequestered jurors stay at a nearby hotel every night until the trial ends. Because news reports or movie plots could affect their verdict, they are not allowed to read newspapers or magazines or watch any television programs that might influence them.

Small-Claims Trials

Are there trials that do not have juries? Yes! These trials take place in small-claims court. They do not use lawyers, either. The plaintiffs and defendants speak for themselves. Plaintiffs can sue defendants for up to a certain amount, usually about $5,000. Examples of small-claims cases include unpaid rent, damaged property, or incomplete services, such as those performed by building contractors. Both parties present their sides before a **magistrate**, who decides which party wins the case.

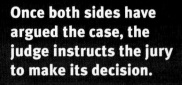

Once both sides have argued the case, the judge instructs the jury to make its decision.

CHAPTER 5

Reaching a Verdict

The jury's final duty is the verdict. The jurors review the evidence and vote. In a criminal trial, they vote "guilty" or "not guilty." In a civil trial, they vote in favor of the plaintiff or the defendant. In most cases, the verdict must be **unanimous**. In a civil trial, the plaintiff and defendant can choose to accept a majority vote if all the jury members do not agree.

 In some states, judges can be called for jury duty.

Deliberation Begins

After the evidence has been presented, the judge gives the jurors instructions and then excuses them to discuss the case privately. This meeting is called a **deliberation**. A deliberation is finished when the jurors have decided which side they rule in favor of. This is called reaching a verdict.

During deliberation, jurors carefully analyze the information given to them during the trial.

The foreperson helps lead discussions during deliberation.

Follow the Leader

Each jury must select a foreperson as its leader.
The foreperson leads the deliberation and keeps
track of the jury's votes. The foreperson's job
can be very difficult. Sometimes jury members
argue with each other because they disagree
on the verdict. The foreperson must settle these
arguments and keep order during deliberation.

A jury that cannot reach a verdict is called a hung jury.

The foreperson delivers the verdict to the judge.

Decisions, Decisions

Reaching a unanimous decision is not always easy. A jury may deliberate for a few hours or for several days. When a verdict is reached, the foreperson sends a message to the judge. Everyone returns to the courtroom. The foreperson might read the verdict aloud. Other times, he or she writes the verdict down and gives it to the court clerk, who reads it aloud.

Case Closed

Shortly after the verdict is read, the judge thanks the jury and allows its members to leave. Now that the trial has ended, jurors are finally allowed to talk about the case. However, they are required never to reveal how the other jurors voted. No matter what type of trial a juror participates in, citizens should feel proud to have fulfilled this important responsibility. ★

After the trial, the jurors are once again free to discuss the case, read newspapers, and watch the news.

True Statistics

Parts of the U.S. Constitution that guarantee trials by jury: Sixth and Seventh Amendments

Estimated number of jury trials in the United States each year: 154,000

Percentage of civil cases that actually go to trial: 2

Number of U.S. states that require verdicts to be unanimous in civil trials: 19

Number of U.S. states that require verdicts to be unanimous in felony (a type of criminal) trials: 48

Number of U.S. states that require verdicts to be unanimous in misdemeanor (a type of criminal) trials: 49

Amount of money prospective jurors are paid for jury duty: $5 to $50 per day

Possible penalties for failing to report for jury duty: Fine; temporary loss of driver's license; imprisonment

Did you find the truth?

(T) A person must be at least 18 years old to serve as a juror.

(F) A juror can use social media during a trial.

Resources

Books

Cheney, Lynne. *We the People: The Story of Our Constitution*. New York: Simon & Schuster Books for Young Readers, 2008.

Furgang, Kathy. *The Seventh Amendment: The Right to a Jury Trial*. New York: Rosen Central Publishing, 2011.

Kowalski, Kathiann M. *Order in the Court: A Look at the Judicial Branch*. Minneapolis: Lerner Publications Company, 2004.

Taylor-Butler, Christine. *The Supreme Court*. New York: Children's Press, 2008.

Visit this Scholastic Web site for more information on juries:
★ www.factsfornow.scholastic.com
Enter the keyword **Jury**

Important Words

biased (BYE-uhst) — prejudiced, or favoring one person or point of view more than another

defendant (di-FEN-duhnt) — the person in a court case who has been accused or who is being sued

deliberation (duh-lib-ur-AY-shuhn) — a meeting that is held to consider something carefully

magistrate (MAJ-i-strate) — a government official who can act as a judge in court

naturalized (NACH-ur-uh-lized) — made a citizen of a country where one was not born

plaintiff (PLAYN-tif) — the side in a court case that has been wronged

potential (puh-TEN-shuhl) — possible, but not yet actual or real

prosecutor (PRAH-si-kyoo-tur) — the lawyer who represents the plaintiff

sequestered (suh-KWEST-urd) — kept separate; not allowed to go home at the end of each day while a trial is taking place

unanimous (yoo-NAN-uh-muhs) — agreed on by everyone

verdict (VUR-dikt) — the decision a jury reaches in a trial

voir dire (VWAR DEER) — the initial questioning of a potential juror by a judge or lawyers

Index

Page numbers in **bold** indicate illustrations

About the Author

Sarah De Capua is the author of many nonfiction books for children. She enjoys helping young readers learn about our country through civics education. She has been called for jury duty three times but has never actually been chosen as a trial juror. De Capua works as a children's book author and editor, as well as a college composition instructor. She holds a master's degree in teaching from Sacred Heart University in Connecticut, and is currently working toward her doctorate in composition and TESOL at Indiana University of Pennsylvania. She has written other True Books in this set, including *Voting*, *Paying Taxes*, and *Running for Public Office*.